T0088161

It's fun to draw
Fairies, Mermaids,
Princesses,
and Ballerinas

It's fun to draw Fairies, Mermaids, Princesses, and Ballerinas

Mark Bergin

Sky Pony Press
New York

Mark Bergin was born in Hastings, England. He has illustrated an award-winning series and written over twenty books. He has done many book designs, layouts, and storyboards in many styles including cartoon for numerous books, posters, and advertisements. He lives in Bexhill-on-sea with his wife and three children.

HOW TO USE THIS BOOK:
Start by following the numbered splats on the left-hand page. These steps will ask you to add some lines to your drawing. The new lines are always drawn in red so you can see how the drawing builds from step to step. Read the "You can do it!" splats to learn about drawing and coloring techniques you can use.

Copyright © 2019 by Mark Bergin

All Rights Reserved. No part of this book may be reproduced in any manner without the express written consent of the publisher, except in the case of brief excerpts in critical reviews or articles. All inquiries should be addressed to Sky Pony Press, 307 West 36th Street, 11th Floor, New York, NY 10018.

Sky Pony Press books may be purchased in bulk at special discounts for sales promotion, corporate gifts, fund-raising, or educational purposes. Special editions can also be created to specifications. For details, contact the Special Sales Department, Sky Pony Press, 307 West 36th Street, 11th Floor, New York, NY 10018 or info@skyhorsepublishing.com.

Sky Pony® is a registered trademark of
Skyhorse Publishing, Inc.®, a Delaware corporation.

Visit our website at www.skyponypress.com.

10 9 8 7 6 5 4 3 2

This product conforms to CPSIA 2008

Library of Congress Cataloging-in-Publication Data is available on file

Cover design by Daniel Brount
Cover illustration by Mark Bergin
ISBN: 978-1-5107-4362-5
Printed in China

Contents

Contents

It's fun to draw Fairies, Mermaids, Princesses, and Ballerinas

Coral, a mermaid

1 Start with a circle for the head. Add a mouth, a nose, and dots for the eyes.

2 Draw in the bodice, arms, and mirror.

3 Add the hair, tiara, bracelet, and reflection.

you can do it!

Use thin felt-tip markers for the lines and thicker felt-tip markers to color in shapes.

4 Draw in her tail.

9

Buttercup, a fairy

1 Start with the head. Add a nose, a mouth, and dots for eyes.

2 Draw in the dress.

you can do it!
Use a felt-tip marker for the lines. Add color with oil pastels. Use your finger to smudge the colors.

Splat-a-fact!
Woodland fairies look after the flowers and trees, with the help of the small creatures who live there.

3 Add the arms and legs.

4 Draw in two wings and her hair.

Pearl, a mermaid

1 Start with the head, the mouth, and a a dot for the eye.

2 Add the hair and tiara.

you can do it!
Use pencil for the outlines, then paint in watercolor. Add colored inks to the wet paint for texture.

Splat-a-fact!
Mermaids and mermen have lived in the ocean since the beginning of time.

3 Draw in the bodice and arms.

4 Add her tail.

5 Finish the drawing, adding a crab and rock.

sparkle, the Tooth Fairy

1 Start with the head. Add a mouth, a nose, and dots for the eyes.

2 Add the hair.

3 Draw in the dress.

you can do it!
Use a felt-tip marker for the outline. Add color using crayons.

4 Add the arms and legs.

Splat-a-fact!
The tooth fairy collects children's baby teeth and leaves a gift in return.

5 Draw in wings, a wand, and a bow in the hair.

14

sandy, a mermaid

1 Cut out the head. Add a mouth and eye and glue them down.

you can do it!
Cut out the shapes from colored paper. Glue these onto to a sheet of blue paper. Use a felt-tip marker for the lines.

2 Cut out the hair. Glue down.

MAKE SURE YOU GET AN ADULT TO HELP YOU WHEN USING SCISSORS!

3 Cut out the arms and chest. Glue down.

4 Cut out a long green tail, a flower, and some beads. Glue down.

Splat-a-fact!

Mermaids often
come to the rescue of
shipwrecked sailors.

17

Bubbles, a mermaid

1 Start with the head. Add the nose, mouth, and dots for the eyes.

2 Draw in the body and tail.

you can do it!
Use a felt-tip marker for the outlines. Scribble the colors with various colored oil pastels.

3 Add the hair, necklace, and bikini top.

4 Add the arms and hands.

splat-a-fact!
"The Little Mermaid" is
a story written by Hans
Christian Andersen.

Poppy, the Flower Fairy

1 Start with the head. Add a nose, a mouth, and dots for the eyes.

2 Add the dress.

you can do it!
Use a graphite stick for the lines. Add ink washes. Sponge inks on or add a second colored ink on top of an area that is still wet for extra effects.

Splat-a-fact!
There are fairies all around us, but they are so small that only children can see them.

3 Draw in the arms and legs.

4 Add hair, wings, and a collar.

Princess Oceana

1 Start with the head. Add the mouth and two dots for the eyes.

you can do it!
Use crayons for texture and paint over it with watercolor paint. Use a felt-tip marker for the lines.

2 Add the body, bikini top, and beads.

3 Draw in the hair and a crown.

4 Draw the long, curved tail.

5 Add the arms.

Mermaids keep their tails shiny by rubbing them daily with seaweed.

23

Melody, a mermaid

1 Start with the head. Add a nose, a mouth, and two dots for the eyes.

2 Add her hair.

you can do it!
Draw the outline with a felt-tip marker and color it in with pastel pencils.

Splat-a-fact!
Mermaids can live for 300 years.

3 Add the bodice and beads.

4 Draw in the arms and hands holding a harp with four strings.

5 Add the tail and a rock.

The Fairy Princess

1 Cut out the wings. Glue down.

you can do it!

Cut out shapes from colored paper. Glue them onto a sheet of paper as shown. Use a felt-tip marker for the face.

2 Cut out the hair and a dress. Glue down.

3 Cut out the head and arms. Glue down. Add a nose, a mouth, and eyes with a felt-tip marker.

4 Cut out a crown, the legs, and shoes. Glue down.

26

Splat-a-fact!
A "fairy ring" is a circle of toadstools where the fairies gather to dance.

MAKE SURE
YOU GET AN
ADULT TO HELP
YOU WHEN
USING SCISSORS!

Holly, the Christmas Fairy

1 Start with an oval for the head. Add eyes, a nose, and a mouth.

You can do it!
Use crayons for texture and paint over it with watercolor paint. Use a felt-tip marker for the lines.

2 Add the shape of the hair.

3 Draw the body and dress.

4 Add arms holding a present.

5 Draw the legs and feet.

6 Add bows to the hair and present.

7 Finish by adding the wings.

Splat-a-fact!

Titania, Queen of the fairies, lives in a fairy castle with her husband, King Oberon.

29

Pebbles, a mermaid

1 Start with the head. Add a nose, a mouth, and dots for eyes.

2 Add the hair and beads.

3 Draw in the bodice and tail.

4 Add the arms and the rock.

5 Draw in her hair clip and comb.

you can do it!
Use a felt-tip marker for the lines. Add color using chalky pastels. Use your fingers to blend the colors.

Splat-a-fact!
Mermaids are beautiful creatures that are halfhuman and half fish.

Twinkle, a fairy

1 Start with the head. Add the nose, mouth, and dots for the eyes.

2 Draw in the neck and hair.

3 Add the dress.

you can do it!
Use markers to fill in the background and to add color details. Use a felt-tip marker for the lines.

Splat-a-fact!
A fairy always carries a pinch of magic dust to help with her spells.

4 Draw in arms and legs.

5 Add a wand and wings.

32

Ella, the Dust Fairy

1 Start with the head. Add a mouth, a nose, and two dots for the eyes.

2 Add the dress.

3 Draw in the hair and arms.

you can do it!
Use crayons to create patterns and texture. Paint over it with watercolor paints. Use a felt-tip marker for the lines.

4 Draw in the feather and the legs.

5 Add two wings.

34

Splat-a-fact!

Not all fairies have wings. Some fairies don't fly at all.

Princess Anna

1 Start with the head. Add a nose, mouth, and dots for eyes.

2 Add the arms and the top.

3 Draw in the hair and crown.

Splat-a-fact!
Princesses often live in castles.

3 Add the dress and the feet.

you can do it!
Use a felt-tip marker for the lines and add color using colored pencils. Use the pencils in a scribbly way to add texture.

36

Louise

1 Start with the head. Add a nose, mouth, and dots for eyes.

2 Add the hair and an ear.

you can do it!
Use a brown felt-tip marker for the lines and add color using pencils.

3 Draw in the dress.

splat-a-fact!
Ballerinas have to work hard and practice every day.

4 Add the arms and legs.

5 Add the dress details and a bow.

Henrietta

1 Start with the head. Add a nose, mouth, and dots for eyes.

2 Add the hair.

3 Draw in the tutu top and a big circle for the skirt.

You can do it!
Use crayons for all textures and paint over with watercolor paint. Use a blue felt-tip marker for the lines.

4 Add the legs.

5 Draw the arms.

Splat-a-fact!
Ballerinas can wear out 2 to 3 pairs of point shoes in one week.

Princess Margot

1 Start with the head. Add the nose, mouth, and dots for the eyes.

you can do it!
Use crayons for all textures and paint over using colored inks. Sponge some of the inks for added texture.

2 Add the dress.

3 Draw in the arms and the feet.

4 Add the crown and the hair.

5 Draw in the details of the dress.

42

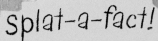

Once upon a time a princess befriended a frog. Then the frog turned into a handsome prince!

43

Princess Lisa

1 Start with the head. Add a nose, mouth, and dots for eyes.

2 Add hair and a crown.

Splat-a-fact!
Princesses have a different dress for each day of the year.

3 Draw in the top.

4 Add the arms and a handbag.

you can do it!
Use crayons for all textures and paint over with watercolors. Sponge some of the paint for added texture.

5 Draw the dress and feet.

44

Marina

1 Cut out the head and glue down. Draw on a mouth and a dot for the eye.

2 Cut out the tutu top and glue down. Cut out the skirt shape and glue down.

You can do it!

Start with a piece of colored paper for the background. Cut out shapes for the spotlight and floor. Glue them down. Now cut out all the shapes for the ballerina and glue them down in the order shown.

Splat-a-fact!

A tutu can take about 60 to 70 hours to make.

3 Cut out the legs and feet. Glue the legs down first, then add shoes.

4 Cut out the hair and glue down. Cut out the arms and glue down.

MAKE SURE YOU GET AN ADULT TO HELP YOU WHEN USING SCISSORS!

Princess Helena

1 Start with the head. Add a mouth and a dot for the eye.

2 Add the hair and crown.

3 Draw in three circles for the top.

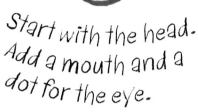

splat-a-fact!
Princesses appear in lots of fairy tales.

4 Add the arms.

you can do it!
Use crayons for the color and a blue felt-tip marker for the lines.

5 Draw the dress and feet.

Princess Melissa

1 Start with the head. Add a nose, mouth, and dots for eyes.

2 Draw in the dress.

3 Add the arms.

Splat-a-fact!
Princesses don't usually do their own laundry.

you can do it!
Use a colored pencil for the lines and add color using watercolor paint.

4 Draw in the ropes and the swing. Add the feet.

5 Add the hair and crown.

Jennifer

1 Start with a head. Add a nose, mouth, and dots for eyes.

2 Add the hair.

3 Draw in the dress.

you can do it!
Add color using colored pencils. Use a black felt-tip marker for the lines, the shoes, and the pattern on the tutu.

4 Add the arms and legs.

5 Shade in the dress and shoes.

splat-a-fact!
Ballerinas need to have strong ankles and knees.

52

Princess Nicole

1 Start with the head. Add a nose, mouth, and lines for eyes.

2 Draw in the top of the dress.

3 Add the rest of the dress.

you can do it!
Use a felt-tip marker for the lines and add color using colored pencils. Use the pencils in a scribbly way to add texture.

splat-a-fact!
Princesses need lots of mattresses.

4 Add the arms and feet.

5 Draw in the hair and crown.

Princess Heather

1 Start with the head. Add a nose, mouth, and dots for eyes.

2 Add the hair.

3 Add the hat and veil.

you can do it!
Use a green felt-tip marker for the lines and add color using watercolor paint.

splat-a-fact!
A princess has everything she wants—beautiful dresses, handbags, tiaras, and jewels.

5 Add the skirt and the feet.

4 Draw in the arms and sleeves.

Amanda

1 Start with the head. Add a nose, mouth, and dots for eyes.

2 Add the hair and ears.

3 Draw in the tutu.

you can do it!

Use a purple felt-tip marker for the lines and add color using colored markers.

4 Add the arms and legs.

splat-a-fact!

Dancing "en pointe" is performed by standing on the tips of your toes.

5 Finish off the details on the tutu.

Kirsten

1 Start with the head. Add a nose, mouth, and dots for eyes.

2 Add the hair.

3 Draw in the tutu.

you can do it!

Use a purple felt-tip marker for the lines and add color with soft, chalky pastels. Smudge and blend some of the colors to add texture.

splat-a-fact!

"Pas de deux" means a dance for two.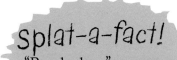

4 Add the arms and legs.

5 Finish off the details of the dress. Add a hairband.

Fiona

1 Start with the head. Add a mouth, nose, and a dot for the eye.

2 Add the hair.

3 Draw in the tutu.

you can do it!
Use crayons to add color and a blue felt-tip marker for the lines. Smudge or blend the color for more texture.

4 Add the legs.

5 Draw in the arms.

splat-a-fact!
It can take over 100 yards of tulle to make a tutu.

Index